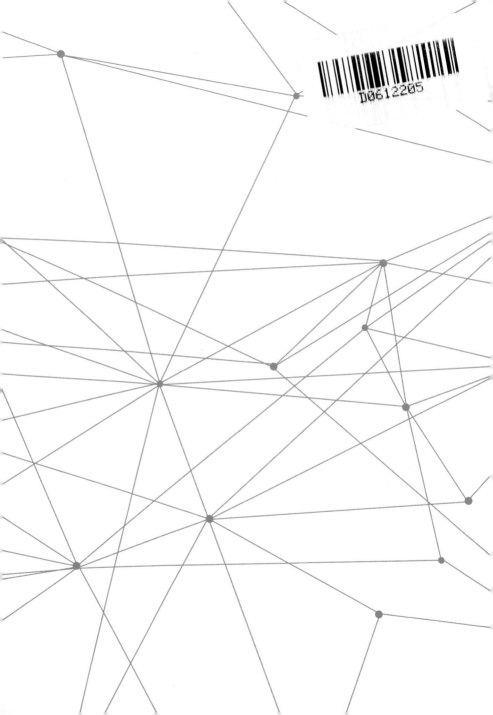

Wired
Published by Orange
a division of The reThink Group, Inc.
5870 Charlotte Lane, Suite 300
Cumming, GA 30040 U.S.A.

The Orange logo is a registered trademark of The reThink Group, Inc.

All Scripture quotations, unless otherwise noted, are taken from the Holy Bible, New International Version®. NIV®. Copyright © 1973, 1978, 1984 by International Bible Society. Used by permission of Zondervan.

Other Orange products are available online and direct from the publisher.
Visit our website at www.ThinkOrange.com for more resources like these.

ISBN: 9781941259504

©2015 The reThink Group

Writers: Rodney Anderson, Sarah Anderson
Lead Editor: Lauren Terrell
Editing Team: Crystal Chiang, Susan Gaines, Kristen Ivy, Mike Jeffries
Art Direction: Ryan Boon
Project Manager: Cody Goshert
Designer: Sharon van Rossum

Printed in the United States of America
First Edition 2015

1 2 3 4 5 6 7 8 9 10

10/15/2015

Copies of this book are available for distribution in churches, schools, and other venues at a significant quantity discount. For more details, go to www.OrangeStore.org.

WIRED

A 4-WEEK DEVOTIONAL EXPERIENCE FOR STUDENTS

RODNEY & SARAH ANDERSON

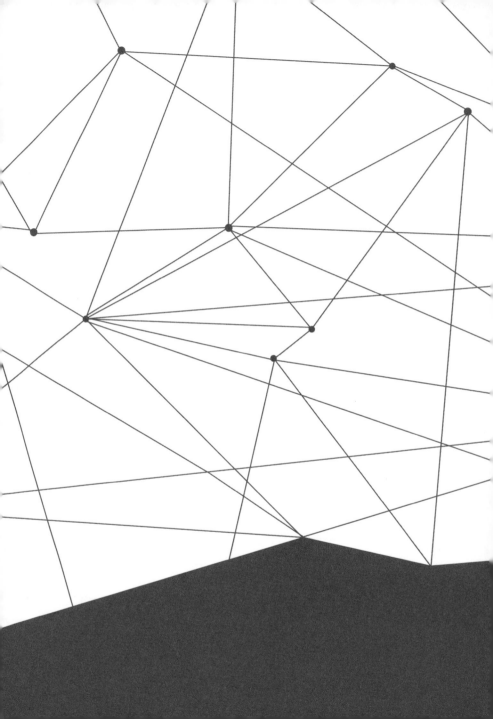

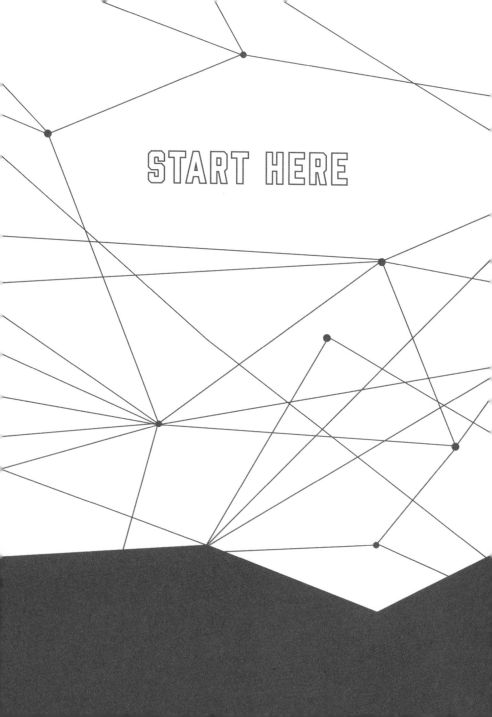

START HERE

DEFYING THE LAWS OF MOTION

Have you ever heard of Sir Isaac Newton?

He's the guy responsible for "discovering" gravity. (Of course, it was there all the time. He's just the one who first realized how everything on Earth is wired to hang out near the ground and not just float around.)

He also wrote what came to be known as "Newton's Three Laws of Motion"—something you learn about in Physics. (Don't worry. This book isn't about that.)

Newton's First Law of Motion says something pretty interesting: "An object at rest stays at rest and an object in motion stays in motion with the same speed and in the same direction unless acted upon by an unbalanced force."

(Have you fallen asleep yet?)

WAKE UP!

All **that** means is: **things are designed, or *wired*, to keep doing what they are already doing.** You probably already knew that.

It's the reason . . .

> it's harder to get up for a snack once you're on the couch, than if you had gotten a snack before you sat down.

it's easier to add a mile to your three-mile run, than it is to get out of bed and force yourself to exercise in the first place.

it's easier to break curfew a third and fifth time, than it is to break it the first.

It's always harder to change what you're already doing, than to keep doing what you've always been doing.

That's where this book comes in.

When you decided to pick up this book—when you decided to try spending some one-on-one time with God—you proved Newton wrong. Well, maybe not wrong. But you showed that while it's easier to keep doing what you're doing, it is possible to do something new.

So **congratulations**! By cracking the cover—by choosing to spend ten minutes of your day in a new way—you are training yourself to try something *new*. That's a big deal.

But it's more than that, too.

You're investing in the most important relationship you could ever have.

You're starting a quest to answer some of the biggest questions you'll ever ask.

You're on your way to learning more about how you are wired and why that even matters.

Maybe that sounds totally overwhelming, because this God stuff is new to you. Or maybe it's not new. You're just beginning to wonder what all of it has to do with you.

Either way, the goal over the next four weeks is to uncover some of the basics of how you are wired when it comes to:

CONNECTING WITH GOD, LOVING YOUR LIFE, EMBRACING COMMUNITY, AND SERVING OTHERS.

When you get to the end, you won't have all the answers. That's a good thing. Figuring out how God wired the world and everything in it may take more than a few short weeks. But you will have the building blocks for a relationship with God, yourself, and the world around you.

That's a great place to start.

So, are you ready to defy the laws of motion?

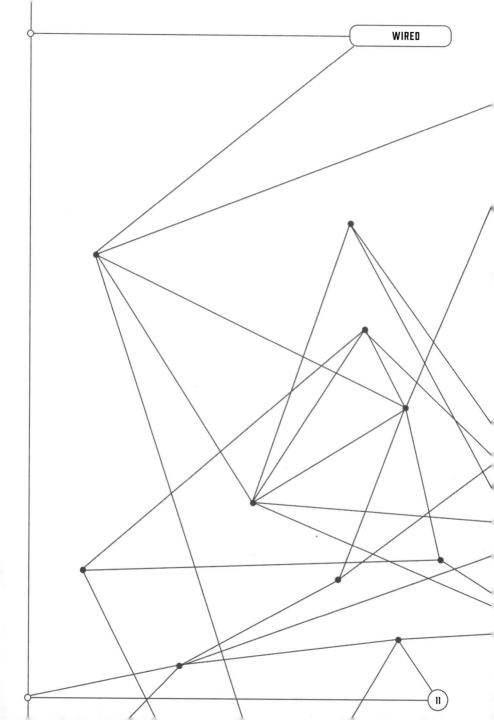

WEEK ONE
CONNECT WITH GOD

CONNECT WITH GOD

What's the first thing that comes to mind when you hear someone say the word

"GOD"?

You may have images that come to mind.

You may think of a word or two.

But when it comes to God, most of us just have questions.

BIG questions:

>   **Who** is God?
>
>   **Where** is God?
>
>   *Is God even real?*

And biggest of all:

If He is real, how am I supposed to connect with this God I cannot see, touch, or hear?

It's true, right? Maybe you've heard it your whole life. Maybe you go to church or you're around Christians and you hear how great He is—how He loves you and how He made you. You hear how He wants to connect with you. But there's one problem nobody seems to mention: you can't see Him. Does that bother anybody else?

How can you connect with Someone—Some**thing**—that is completely **invisible**?

You can't.

But maybe God isn't completely invisible.

YOU ARE WIRED TO CONNECT WITH GOD.

He knows it's hard to connect with someone you can't talk to or FaceTime with—someone you can't **see**.

Maybe that's why He has wired us to see Him, notice Him, and **connect with Him** in other ways.

Connecting with God is about learning to pay attention—to take notice of Him and how He shows up all around you.

As you do, you may just find He is more visible than you ever imagined.

· DAY ONE ·
CREATION

Mexican food is heavenly in all forms. The chips . . . the cheese . . . the tortillas . . . the cilantro . . .

That is, unless you happen to be part of the nearly 14 percent of the population that associates cilantro with the taste of soap.[1]

That's right. Some 900 *million* people out there think almost all Mexican food tastes like *soap*.

Scientists blame genetics. They claim those who have this more-than-slightly bizarre reaction when they eat cilantro share a group of receptor genes that pick up a certain chemical—a chemical found in both cilantro . . . and soap. Go figure.

One food. Two opposite reactions.

But when you think about it, it's not that uncommon. Whether it's food, a movie, a book, or a song, we can all hear the same information, have the same experience, and draw completely opposite conclusions.

Circle one:

COKE or PEPSI?

MARVEL or DC?

iPHONE or ANDROID?

While some debates will never be settled, there *are* things we can all agree on—things that cause the same reaction no matter your genetic makeup.

For example, have you ever seen someone post a picture of a sunset, a storm coming in over the ocean, or the view from a mountaintop and thought, "Gross"?

For some reason, creation doesn't get conflicting opinions.

Whether you categorize yourself as outdoorsy or not, the beauty in nature has the ability to grab your attention like other things can't.

> The way the sun hits the clouds
>
> The way lightning can make designs in the sky
>
> A clear night and a rising moon
>
> Leaves in the Fall
>
> Ocean waves that grow and then crash on the beach

They catch your attention. And you aren't weird for noticing. You are **wired** to notice.

WHAT'S SOMETHING IN NATURE THAT CONSISTENTLY GRABS YOUR ATTENTION?

_____

_____

_____

In his letter to the Romans, a follower of Jesus named Paul writes,

For ever since the world was created, people have seen the earth and sky. Through everything God made, they can clearly see His invisible qualities—His eternal power and divine nature. So they have no excuse for not knowing God. (Romans 1:20 NLT)

Yes, God Himself is invisible. That's no secret. But look out the window. Look at God's vast creation. Paul says you can "*clearly see His invisible qualities*" when you notice all God has created.

God's dependability is visible in tall and sturdy mountains.

God's power is visible in dark and stormy skies.

God's attention to detail is visible in bright and colorful patterns covering everything from a butterfly's wings to a snake's scales.

Too often, God feels invisible and distant. But when we *take the time to notice*, **God is visible in creation**. What you see around you reveals a Creator you can't see.

Life is busy. We rush from school to practice to work and barely have time to sleep in between. Our eyes gravitate to phones, computers, TVs, and video games. It's easy to go a whole day—maybe even a whole week—without pausing to focus our eyes and our thoughts on something not man-made.

WHEN WAS THE LAST TIME YOU NOTICED GOD'S CREATION? WHAT DID YOU NOTICE?

_____

_____

_____

You are wired to notice beautiful things.

You are created to admire God's creation.

You are made to connect with God by connecting with what He made.

Seeing God in creation requires action on your part. Action as big as a long technology-free camping weekend or as small as looking out the car window on your way to school. Sometimes it doesn't take much—just a glimpse—to be reminded that **God is visible in creation**.

FOR TODAY, START WITH TAKING A WALK. OR IF IT'S STORMY, LOOK OUT THE WINDOW. LEAVE TECHNOLOGY BEHIND FOR 10 MINUTES AND *LOOK FOR GOD IN THE PLACES YOU SEE EVERY DAY BUT DON'T ALWAYS NOTICE.* AS YOU LOOK, TAKE NOTE OF GOD'S CHARACTER TRAITS THAT STAND OUT TO YOU IN HIS CREATION. WHEN YOU ARE DONE, WRITE DOWN YOUR OBSERVATIONS HERE:

_____

_____

_____

_____

_____

_____

_____

· DAY TWO ·
WONDERFULLY MADE

When you were first born, there wasn't much on your radar other than . . .

eating.

sleeping.

pooping.

Anything that didn't involve those things didn't really interest you.

But about two months in, everything changed when you began to see things in greater detail. You could spend hours staring at your crib mobile, your ceiling fan, or even at your own hands.

In fact, at one point in your life, those five fingers were very likely the most interesting things you'd ever seen.

Now that you're grown, the fascination has worn off a little. You look in the mirror and see one mouth, a nose, a couple of ears and don't think too much about it.

But maybe if you knew exactly what you were looking at—maybe if you truly understood the complexity of what you see in the mirror —you would revert back to your two-month-old self in a state of total fascination.

You ready to have your mind blown? Great.

Your body—eyes, nose, ears, hands, feet—is made up of somewhere between 37 and 75 *trillion* cells.

Not impressed?

Maybe you don't quite understand how big the number 75 trillion is. Think about it this way: it takes about two weeks to count to a million, around 32 *years* to count to a billion, and approximately 31,000 years to count to a trillion. So you are looking in the neighborhood of 2.3 *million* years to count every cell in your body. *And* each and every cell is artfully crafted by God Himself.

YOUR BODY IS BEYOND COMPLEX.

But it doesn't always feel that way does it?

You wake up every day and see the same person in the mirror. Sure, a few things change from time to time. One day your hair works with you perfectly. The next day you wear a hat. One day you have a new zit on your chin. The next day it's on your forehead. But for the most part, you get used to yourself and hardly pause to think of the complexity and awesomeness God put into the trillions of cells in your body.

It's frustrating when you can't see God—when you feel like He is distant and invisible. But when you understand every cell of your body is God's personal artwork, you can *see* God in *you*.

How cool is that? **God is visible in *you*.**

Thousands of years ago, King David was wowed by God's amazing work. Here's what he wrote:

For you created my inmost being; you knit me together in my mother's womb. I praise you because I am fearfully and wonderfully made; your works are wonderful, I know that full well. (Psalms 139:13-14)

David got what a lot of us seem to miss: That every part of him—his hands, his arms, his face, the hairs on his head—was made by God. He wasn't an accident, an afterthought, or an oversight. He was a work of art. God made King David and that same God made *you*.

And when He made you, God gave you His creativity, His sense of humor, His curiosity, His kindness. **God's artistry and His work are on full display in you.**

WHAT IF EVERY TIME YOU SAW YOURSELF YOU SAW THE WORK OF GOD? HOW WOULD IT CHANGE WHAT YOU BELIEVE ABOUT YOURSELF?

_____

_____

HOW WOULD IT CHANGE THE WAY YOU THINK OF GOD?

_____

_____

TAKE A FEW MINUTES AND WRITE DOWN A REMINDER THAT GOD IS VISIBLE IN <u>YOU</u>. MAYBE IT'S THE VERSE DAVID WROTE IN PSALM 139:13-14. MAYBE IT'S A SIMPLE PHRASE LIKE, "I AM GOD'S PERSONAL WORK OF ART." WHATEVER IT IS, WRITE IT OUT ON A PIECE OF PAPER. THEN TAPE IT TO A MIRROR YOU LOOK AT EVERY DAY TO REMEMBER WHEN YOU FEEL AS IF GOD IS DISTANT AND INVISIBLE, HE IS ACTUALLY AS CLOSE AS THE TRILLIONS OF CELLS IN YOUR BODY. AND THAT IS SOMETHING WORTHY OF FASCINATION.

· DAY THREE ·
THE IMAGE OF GOD

As homecoming queen and senior class president at her high school in Brentwood, Tennessee, Katie Davis had the world before her.

She could go to college.

She could marry her high school boyfriend.

She could take a year off and get a job.

But after spending Christmas break of her senior year on a short-term mission trip to Uganda, she decided to leave every familiar thing behind and permanently move to Africa. Over seven years later, she has started a school in Uganda serving more than 700 kids and a meal program that feeds over a thousand people every day. As if that isn't enough to juggle, Katie and her husband have adopted 13 foster kids in Uganda (so far).[2]

Stories like Katie's stop us in our tracks. When we see people going to great lengths to care for, serve, and love others, it amazes us. Every time.

You've probably heard some "Katie-like" stories in your own world. Maybe no one you know is moving to Uganda, but you've heard stories of people being so outrageously *selfless*, you can't help but be drawn to them.

Maybe you saw a popular kid in your school eating lunch with the socially awkward new kid, despite the eye-rolling and snickering coming from the popular table.

Maybe you watched as your church raised money for some neighbors who lost everything in a house fire.

Maybe you took note as your mom cooked weekly meals for a family with a kid who's really sick.

Or maybe someone did something for you. Someone reached out to you when you felt out of place. Someone forgave you when you acted cruelly. Someone told you they believe in you when you didn't feel like you had much to offer.

WHAT IS ONE ACT OF GREAT KINDNESS OR SELFLESSNESS YOU REMEMBER SEEING OR EXPERIENCING?

_____

_____

_____

_____

No matter the circumstance, we've either received kindness ourselves or watched kindness from other people. And no matter how big or small the act, it stuck with us.

Why is that?

Well, it has something to do with the way we are made—the way we are *wired*.

The book of Genesis begins with the story of how the world (and everything in it) was wired. Over and over we see God creating, adding to what He has already made, making more and more complex things, until at the very end, He makes people.

*Then God said, "Let us make mankind in our image, in our likeness, so that they may rule over the fish in the sea and the birds in the sky, over the livestock and all the wild animals, and over all the creatures that move along the ground. **So God created mankind** in His own image, in the image of God He created them; male and female He created them." (Genesis 1:26-27, emphasis added)*

In the rest of creation, we see God's fingerprint. We see a glimpse of His might and creativity in night, day, land, and sea. But we see something bigger entirely when we look at people.

Genesis tells us we have *God's image* in us.

God not only artfully crafted every cell of our bodies, He gave you—and every person you see—HIS ability to love, serve, and encourage others. Just like you may see your grandmother in the way your mom laughs or hear your dad in the way your brother speaks, **when you see people behave a certain way, you see more than just them, you also see God.**

When you see forgiveness, you are seeing God.

When you see compassion, you are seeing God.

When you see selflessness, you are seeing God.

WHEN YOU SEE PEOPLE DOING GOOD THINGS, YOU ARE SEEING THE IMAGE OF A GOOD GOD.

Remember, when you feel God is invisible or too far away to connect with, He may be more places than you ever imagined. **Because God is visible in others**.

The world is full of opportunities to see God at work. And you don't have to be in a church to see Him. When you see the kind deeds of everyday people, whether or not they even believe in God, you are seeing the image of God.

TAKE A FEW MINUTES TO MAKE A LIST OF PEOPLE— CHRISTIAN OR NOT—YOU HAVE SEEN THE IMAGE OF GOD IN. WHICH OF GOD'S QUALITIES SHOWS THROUGH EACH PERSON?

I HAVE SEEN THE IMAGE OF GOD IN:

THE QUALITY WHICH SHOWED THROUGH WAS:

_____   _____

_____   _____

_____   _____

_____   _____

_____   _____

_____   _____

_____   _____

_____   _____

_____   _____

· DAY FOUR ·
JESUS

Several years ago, PBS produced a documentary on the black mamba—one of the world's deadliest snakes—claiming it wasn't as evil as people believed. After all, it allows a good 45 minutes after it bites its victim before the two drops of venom kills them. (See? It's practically a humanitarian!) The show suggested the black mamba isn't all bad, it's just *misunderstood*.

Nice try, PBS. We're not buying it.

The black mamba really is as terrible as people believe. No misunderstanding there. But *actual* misunderstandings are a part of life. They happen all the time. And when you don't have the whole story, your imagination fills in the blanks. That's when things can get complicated.

You read part of a text over your brother's shoulder and jump to a conclusion without hearing the whole story.

You find out all your friends got together but didn't invite you . . . without realizing they were planning a surprise party for you.

HAVE YOU EVER BEEN MISUNDERSTOOD? WHAT HAPPENED? HOW DID YOU CLEAR UP THE CONFUSION?

_____

_____

The problem with following a God we can't see, touch, or hear is that sometimes it feels like our entire understanding of Him is blank spaces waiting to be filled in. And with so much uncertainty, we can easily misunderstand what God is really like. We might get an idea that He's one way when things are going really well in our lives, but when things are tough, we find ourselves thinking maybe He's not who we thought He was.

And so, it's easy to end up with a very mixed up picture of God. It's like when you open a puzzle for the first time and pour all the pieces on the table. Maybe the pieces are all there, maybe you can kind of see how some of it fits together, but the whole picture is unclear.

WHAT THREE WORDS WOULD YOU USE TO DESCRIBE WHAT GOD IS LIKE, BASED ON YOUR EXPERIENCE ALONE?

1.
2.
3.

Truthfully, you aren't the first to feel confused by who God is. The entire Old Testament tells the story of thousands of years of confusion. It talks about the years people spent piecing together ancient stories of God from prophets and kings. And while they were filled with dozens of real ways God showed Himself—burning bushes, talking donkeys, bread falling from the sky—no one was quite clear on what this God was really like.

Then Jesus showed up.

Jesus is important to God's story for a lot of reasons. **But one of the biggest reasons is that Jesus makes our picture of God crystal clear.** The apostle Paul said it this way:

Christ is the visible image of the invisible God. He existed before anything was created and is supreme over all creation.
(Colossians 1:15 NLT)

Jesus answered the question that had nagged people for as long as humanity had been around: **What is God like?**

Jesus came into the world as a physical, *visible* representation of God to clear up any confusion or misunderstandings. Then He wowed everyone with signs and wonders, with wisdom and compassion, with truth and grace, and with *love*.

Want to know what God is like? Look to the one person who was actually God Himself and find that **God is visible in Jesus**.

What we see in Jesus is a God who wants a relationship, a God who's willing to do anything to be close to us, a God who isn't afraid of our mistakes or threatened by our sin. In Jesus, we see God doing whatever it takes to connect with the people He loves. And that includes you. *Especially* you. **In Jesus, God made a way to connect with you, so you can spend your life learning to connect with Him.**

God is visible in Jesus, and because of Jesus we see God is even better than we could imagine.

WHAT THREE WORDS WOULD YOU USE TO DESCRIBE WHAT JESUS IS LIKE?

1.

2.

3.

IF YOU HAVE NO CLUE WHAT JESUS IS LIKE, START WITH READING A FEW CHAPTERS OF THE BOOK OF MATTHEW (IT'S THE FIRST BOOK IN THE NEW TESTAMENT). WHILE YOU READ, KEEP A RUNNING LIST OF JESUS' QUALITIES.

· DAY FIVE ·
WHAT MATTERS MOST

WHAT HAS BEEN YOUR FAVORITE YEAR OF SCHOOL SO FAR AND WHY? _____

_____

Do you remember what school was like in Kindergarten? Whether your favorite year was second grade, fifth grade, or this year, there's no denying Kindergarten was pretty sweet.

Life was so much easier back then.

You showed up at school, did a few minutes of work, took a nap, had a snack break, went to recess, ate lunch, took another nap, did a few more minutes of work, then headed home (presumably for a snack and another nap.) It was a great life!

The worst days in Kindergarten were the days recess got rained out. But even then, you played half the day inside. And the best days of Kindergarten? Show and tell. Hands down.

Show and tell was when you got to bring in something that was special to you. Something like the shell you found over summer break or the hairball your cat coughed up that morning. The items were never *that* impressive but all Kindergarteners love talking about themselves. So, all Kindergarteners love show and tell.

Now that you're older, recess has been replaced by biology class and show and tell time has been replaced by posting pictures of all your cool stuff online.

At any age, we like talking about ourselves—about the things that matter most to us.

But as you get older, you start showing and telling others who you are by the way you live your life and the way you treat other people.

THINK ABOUT THIS FOR A MINUTE. **HOW WOULD YOUR CLOSEST FRIENDS AND FAMILY ANSWER IF YOU ASKED THEM THIS QUESTION: "BASED ON THE THINGS I NORMALLY SAY AND DO, WHAT DO YOU THINK ARE THE THREE MOST IMPORTANT THINGS TO ME?"**

1.

2.

3.

Jesus' teachings are full of great life advice, especially for those who want a relationship with God. But even Jesus Himself was able to narrow all His teachings down to one thing that stood out as more important than all the other things He said.

We call it the Greatest Commandment.

One day, several leaders came to Jesus and asked Him what He thought was the most important religious law. Jesus answered this way:

> "'**Love the Lord your God** with all your heart and with all your soul and with all your mind.' This is the first and greatest commandment. And the second is like it: '**Love your neighbor as yourself**.' All the Law and the Prophets hang on these two commandments."
> (Matthew 22:37-40, emphasis added)

Okay, okay. So He narrowed it down to *two* important things.

1. LOVE GOD.
2. LOVE PEOPLE LIKE YOU LOVE YOURSELF.

If you want to know and follow God, if you want to love Him and have a relationship with Him, the first step is to love other people. You can't do one without the other.

The way you treat people, specifically the way you *love* people, shows and tells them who God is.

How you treat your friends,

how you encourage those on your team,

how you respond when someone treats you unfairly,

how you comfort others through tough times,

sends a message to the world around you.

In that passage, Jesus points out that **God is visible *through* you**.

Your love for God is directly related to your love for others. So what are you showing and telling about your relationship with God?

WHAT DO YOU THINK YOUR ACTIONS TELL OTHERS ABOUT GOD?

_____

_____

_____

WHAT CAN YOU DO TO MAKE GOD MORE VISIBLE TO SOMEONE *TODAY?*

_____

_____

_____

_____

WHAT ABOUT IN THE COMING WEEK?

_____

_____

_____

_____

TRY THIS

Over and over this week, you've seen how **an invisible God isn't as hard to find as you may have thought**. And that's really great news. But what do you do now?

Try carrying this book around with you to make a list of all the ways you *see* evidence of God. Because when you make an effort to notice Him, you'll find yourself connecting to God.

Look outside.

Look at your friends.

Look at what you see displayed in the kindness of strangers.

THEN WRITE IT DOWN.

_____

_____

_____

_____

_____

_____

_____

WHEN YOU TAKE NOTE OF WHERE YOU SEE GOD NOW, YOU'LL HAVE A WAY TO REMEMBER WHAT HE'S LIKE WHEN YOU HAVE A HARD TIME SEEING HIM LATER.

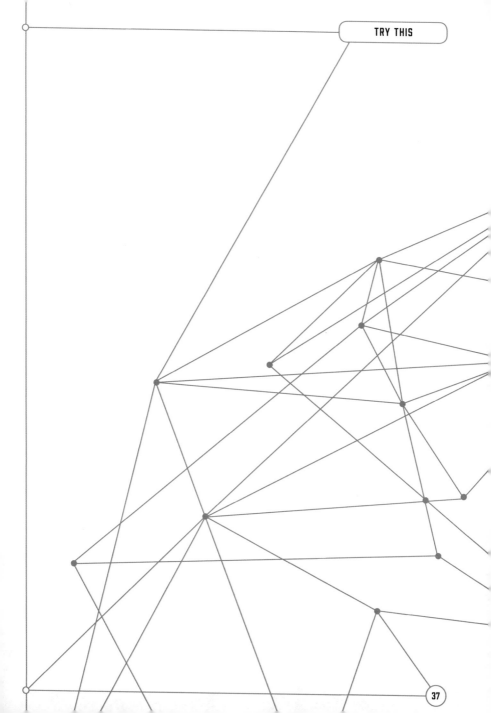

WEEK TWO

LOVE YOUR LIFE

LOVE YOUR LIFE

What do you want to be when you grow up?

Chances are, this question has crossed your mind (or been drilled into it, by every teacher, parent, coach, and babysitter starting at age two).

> Maybe you want to be a history professor at an Ivy League university.
>
> Maybe this week you feel like being a reality TV star.
>
> Maybe you feel lucky just to know what you are going to wear today.

The truth is, it's more than just the overly curious adults in your life who care about the answer to this question. *God does, too.* **But even more than caring what you are going to be when you grow up, God cares *who* you are going to be**—not just when you grow up, but *right now*.

God wants you to be someone who loves life. He wants you to be someone who has discovered how you are wired. Someone who does everything in your power to make the best choices, based on what you know to be true about God and you.

He wants you to be able to look back at these years in your life and say, "That's when I started to *love* who God made me to be, and *live* like I love who God made me to be."

Remember that Scripture you read last week? The commandment Jesus Himself said was the greatest of all commandments? (Feel free to flip back to page 32 or check out Matthew 22:37-39 again.)

Jesus wants us to love God and love people. Last week was all about looking for God, because when we see God, we can better connect with Him. Connecting with God is a great first step in *loving* God—the first part of the Greatest Commandment.

So, what's next? Love people. Except, what Jesus throws in at the very end of that verse in Matthew is a game changer: Love other people *like you love yourself.*

In other words, **before you can understand the best ways to love others, you first have to know what it means to love you**—to love your purpose, your character, your choices, your *life.*

YOU ARE WIRED TO LOVE YOUR LIFE.

That's why we're going to spend the next few days learning how to **love your life**, because when you love *who* you are, you will be better at loving God and loving others.

· DAY ONE ·
YOUR I.D.

Have you ever seen one of those "Found Dog" flyers posted around your neighborhood? They typically have a picture of the dog, followed by about fifteen pieces of crucial information—color, size, weight, age, every freckle, every marking, on and on and on. These days those flyers are fewer and fewer because of a microchip about the size of a grain of rice.[3]

That microchip is like a permanent embedded collar. Each cat or dog is given a chip with one tiny piece of information on it. An I.D. number. That's it. No name, no address, no age. When that number is scanned, that's when the magic happens. That one number will bring up all the information needed to locate a lost pet's home and contact its owner.

That one tiny implant doesn't hold *all* the information about a pet, but it holds the most important information, the part that points to his identity.

What would you say is the most important piece of information about you? Is it your friends? Your family? Your academic performance? Your athletic achievement?

IT'S PROBABLY PRETTY HARD TO COME UP WITH AN ANSWER. BUT TRY TO THINK OF ONE THING THAT MAKES YOU *YOU* AND WRITE IT HERE:

_____

You may be a **_great friend_**. People trust you and confide in you. You remember birthdays and celebrate achievements.

You may be a really **_respectful_** son or daughter. You help around the house and would never intentionally break the rules your parents set.

You may be incredibly **_smart_**, tutoring others who have a hard time in a subject that comes easily to you.

You may be an **_exceptional athlete_**. Your performance carried your school to the state championship.

The problem is, your sense of identity can break down when you have a falling out with your friends, when your family drives you _crazy_, when you don't make the grade you want, or your performance on the court is lacking. When the most important thing about you is wrapped up in any of those things, what begins as just a bad day can become something that really messes with your identity.

In other words, **when your identity is tied to something that changes quickly, your sense of who you are can get quickly shaken.**

HOW DO YOU RESPOND WHEN YOU FEEL LIKE YOU ARE FAILING IN THE ONE THING THAT DEFINES YOU MOST?

_____

_____

_____

_____

So what if there was another way? A way to feel secure and confident in who you are, _all the time_, no matter what's going on around you?

John, one of the disciples of Jesus, gives us insight into how we might do this:

> *How great is the love the Father has lavished on us, that we should be called children of God!* (1 John 3:1)

Your grades matter. Your sports matter. Your friends and your family matter. But none of these things define you. None of these things is the most important thing about you. **The most important thing about you isn't something you do. The most important thing about you is God's love for you**.

That doesn't change. It isn't something you aim for and work towards. It isn't something that adjusts, based on God's mood or your behavior. It's constant. God's love is like that microchip. His love is your I.D. number. The one piece of information that determines who you are, what you are worth, and to whom you belong.

GOD'S LOVE IS THE *ONE* THING ABOUT YOU THAT TELLS *EVERYTHING* ABOUT YOU.

And when you know that piece of information, it's really all you ever need to know. **God's got you.**

When nothing else feels dependable, *God* is.

When nothing else stays the same, *God* does.

YOUR IDENTITY IS TOO IMPORTANT TO BE BUILT ON SOMETHING THAT CAN CHANGE.

God's love doesn't change. The sooner we understand and believe that, the better we will understand ourselves and appreciate the way He made us.

HOW DOES KNOWING THAT GOD'S LOVE IS THE MOST IMPORTANT THING ABOUT YOU CHANGE THE WAY YOU SEE YOURSELF?

_____

_____

_____

_____

_____

_____

_____

_____

_____

· DAY TWO ·
COMPARISON

It wasn't that long ago when hardly anyone knew about social media. Now, it's everywhere. Facebook, Twitter, Instagram, Snapchat, Vine, Periscope, Tumblr, etc. By the time you read this book there will be a dozen new ones. While you may pride yourself on keeping up with the latest and greatest, the number of social media sites that exist worldwide would blow your mind.

What about Petster? It's a networking site for pets and pet owners, with users from all over the world. One of the more popular pets on the site? Mr. Bigglesworth the hamster.

What about Ravelry? It's a network of over three million people who love knitting and crocheting.

In the world of social media, there's a place for even the most unusual people. Everyone can feel like they fit. Except when they don't. Even with all the super-specific groups, social media can still make you feel like an outsider. Like you're lacking in some way. Like everyone else appears to have it together and you don't.

You've probably gotten that feeling when you see everyone else's posts. You *were* happy with your life, until you caught a glimpse of someone else's.

The good news? You're not alone. *Everyone's* in the same boat. *All of us have self-esteem, self-doubt, or insecurity issues to some degree or another.* **All of us have compared ourselves to others at some**

point. And more often than not, when we open social media, all of us are reminded of things we don't really like about ourselves.

WHAT ARE YOUR THREE FAVORITE THINGS ABOUT YOURSELF?

1.

2.

3.

WHAT ARE THREE THINGS YOU WISH YOU COULD CHANGE?

1.

2.

3.

In the book of Proverbs, Solomon writes about the importance of finding confidence even in the things you wish you could change. Solomon—known as the wisest guy (next to Jesus) in the Bible—gives great insight into the danger of comparing yourself to others. Check it out:

> *A peaceful heart leads to a healthy body;*
> *jealousy is like cancer in the bones.*
> (Proverbs 14:30 NLT)

Wow. Did you catch the second part of that verse? Solomon says that jealousy, or comparing yourself to others and what they have, affects you like cancer affects the body.

Just like cancer makes you physically sick from the inside out, comparing yourself to others makes you emotionally sick from the inside out.

WHEN YOU COMPARE YOURSELF TO OTHERS, YOU'RE PLAYING A GAME YOU CAN'T WIN.

You will make yourself miserable wishing you looked like them, or were as athletic as they are, or as popular as they seem to be.

Jealousy eats away at you and makes you miserable. (Chances are you didn't need someone to tell you that. You already knew jealousy wasn't doing you any favors.)

WHAT IS THE NUMBER ONE WAY YOU COMPARE YOURSELF TO OTHERS? WHY?

_____

_____

_____

_____

The good news is Solomon offers an alternative. He tells us that a peaceful heart leads to a healthy life. But what's a "peaceful heart"?

A peaceful heart is . . .

a heart that no longer fights who God made you to be.

a heart that focuses on the qualities you love about yourself.

a heart that knows **God made you to be _you_.**

Is it okay to wish things were different about yourself? Of course. The trouble is that as soon as it becomes the focus of your life, you set yourself up for misery.

LOVING YOUR LIFE BEGINS WHEN YOU LOVE THE PERSON GOD CREATED YOU TO BE. GO BACK AND LOOK AT YOUR THREE FAVORITE QUALITIES ABOUT YOURSELF. MAKE THESE THE HOME SCREEN ON YOUR PHONE OR COMPUTER SO WHEN YOU ARE TEMPTED TO COMPARE YOURSELF, YOU CAN EASILY BE REMINDED OF THE REASONS YOU ARE AT PEACE WITH WHO YOU ARE. THEN SPEND A FEW MINUTES THANKING GOD FOR THE PERSON HE MADE YOU TO BE.

· DAY THREE ·
WHAT YOU THINK ABOUT

Experts say kids begin having dreams with actual plot lines around age seven.[4] Maybe you can remember every vivid detail of your first nightmare. Maybe you still wake up almost every morning wondering why you dreamed your teeth were falling out or you showed up at school in your underwear . . . again. Or maybe you have a nagging feeling you dreamed something, but never can remember what it was.

DO YOU USUALLY REMEMBER YOUR DREAMS?

YES   NO

IF YOU DO, WHAT'S THE CRAZIEST DREAM YOU'VE EVER HAD?

_____

_____

_____

The crazy thing about dreams is, we have _no control_ over them. While our bodies are resting, our minds are creating the most amazing and unlikely stories.

The same can be true when you're awake, right? Whether you are awake or dreaming, it can feel like you have no control over what your brain is thinking. For example, have you ever sat in an English class and no matter how hard you try, you think about almost anything on the planet _except grammar_?

It can feel like you're powerless when it comes to controlling your thoughts. It's like your mind has a mind of its own.

Most of the time, it's harmless. But other times, your thoughts take you to places you don't need to go. Your thoughts go negative. Your mind makes you fearful, angry, or anxious.

When that happens it's easy to end up feeling miserable. Because . . .

THE MORE NEGATIVE YOUR THOUGHTS ARE, THE LESS YOU LOVE YOUR LIFE.

The apostle Paul says we actually do have control over our thoughts, and if we focus our minds in the right direction it can make a huge difference.

> *Finally, brothers, whatever is true, whatever is noble, whatever is right, whatever is pure, whatever is lovely, whatever is admirable—if anything is excellent or praiseworthy—think about such things.*
> (Philippians 4:8)

Paul is telling us to *take control.*

You are not a victim of your thoughts. You are not a bystander. You are steering the ship. In other words, **you need to think about what you think about**. Choose to use the power you have to direct your thoughts towards things that are . . .

True	Lovely
Noble	Admirable
Right	Excellent
Pure	Praiseworthy

Why?

Because **when you look for what is *good*, your life will begin to reflect what is *good*.**

Can you think of someone you know who always seems to focus on the good? Someone who has *trained* their mind to only see the positive? It isn't that nothing challenging ever happens to these people, or that their lives are one good thing after another, or that they live with their heads in the clouds disconnected from the reality of bad things happening. It's that they've learned to **think about what they think about.** It's that they understand when they think about the good, they become more capable of *seeing* the good, even amid the bad. And something about them is *different* because of it.[5]

Right after Paul tells us what to think about, in the very next verse he says,

> *Whatever you have learned or received or heard from me, or seen in me—put it into practice. And the God of peace will be with you.*
> (Philippians 4:9)

The God of *peace*. Peace. The same word that showed up yesterday when Solomon told us what was available when we stopped comparing ourselves with others is also available to you when you begin to **think about what you think about.**

In fact, it sounds like loving your life and *peace* go hand-in-hand.

TAKE A FEW MINUTES NOW TO THINK ABOUT THE GOOD—THE NOBLE, RIGHT, PURE, AND PRAISEWORTHY. THINK ABOUT THE GOOD THINGS IN YOUR OWN LIFE THAT YOU'VE EXPERIENCED LATELY. IT DOESN'T HAVE

TO BE RELIGIOUS OR EARTH-SHATTERING.
NOW WRITE TEN OF THOSE THINGS HERE:

1. _____   6. _____

2. _____   7. _____

3. _____   8. _____

4. _____   9. _____

5. _____   10. _____

Try focusing on the good you experience every day, no matter how small. **Because when you think about what you think about, when you choose to see more good in your life than bad, you will love your life more and be more inclined to thank God for those things**.

NOW TAKE THE NEXT FEW MINUTES TO THANK GOD (OUT LOUD, IN YOUR HEAD, OR ON THE LINES BELOW) FOR SOME OF THE THINGS YOU LISTED ABOVE.

_____

_____

_____

_____

_____

_____

_____

_____

_____

· DAY FOUR ·
WISDOM

THINK OF YOUR FAVORITE DESSERT.

Now picture this: Someone sets a few bites of your favorite dessert on the table in front of you. They tell you if you can resist eating it for 15 minutes, you will get TWO full servings to enjoy.

Then they leave the room.

There you are, mouth watering, all alone with your conscience . . . and a plate of the dessert you would want served with your last meal on Earth. What do you do?

There are actually many hilarious videos out there involving young kids and this exact experiment. One of the funniest involves kids having to resist a perfectly round, sugar-filled marshmallow. And they are always told they will get more than what's in front of them if they can just resist for a few minutes.

It seems simple enough.

But, did we mention . . . MARSHMALLOWS?!?!

That's what the kids are thinking. As soon as the grownup leaves, the hidden camera catches many of them diving right in to the sticky sweet goodness.

Self-control flies right out the window.

Other kids are model citizens. Quietly sitting on their hands, closing their eyes, and doing whatever it takes to restrain themselves.

And then there's the third group that wins for being most entertaining. These kids do what they are told. They don't eat the marshmallow, but guess what? Nobody said anything about *licking* the marshmallow.

It's hilarious to watch these kids get as close to the marshmallow as possible without actually eating it.

WHICH GROUP OF KIDS DO YOU RELATE TO THE MOST IN THIS EXPERIMENT?

_____

Maybe that's why it's so funny, because we can relate. Most people exhaust themselves getting as close as possible to the line of doing something wrong without *quite* crossing over it.

The Bible has a lot to say about how dangerous it is to walk *that* close to the line. In fact, while the Bible has a lot to say about avoiding wrong things and doing the right thing, it also reminds us there's a third option—the *wise* thing.

But, what does that mean?

HOW WOULD YOU DEFINE THE WORD *WISE*?

_____

_____

_____

_____

One way to think of wisdom is this: **Instead of asking, "Is it wrong?" ask, "Is it best?"**

For example, it may not be wrong to leave out some facts when filling your parents in on what happened this weekend. But is it best? Probably not.

The problem is, sometimes we think as long as we are avoiding what's *wrong*, we're doing okay. **But wisdom means choosing what's best, not simply avoiding what's wrong.**

In the book of Proverbs we read,

> The one who gets wisdom **loves life**;
> The one who cherishes understanding will soon prosper.
> (Proverbs 19:8, emphasis added)

This verse doesn't tell us to avoid what's wrong at all costs. It doesn't tell us, "As long as you stay on the right side of the line, you will love life." Because the truth is, you can be on the right side of the line and still be so stressed about toppling over it that you can't actually enjoy life.

This passage is saying if you want to love your life, **wisdom is the best bet.**

Wisdom protects you. Wisdom is smart. Going after wisdom means you are more concerned with making smart choices than just dodging bad ones.

WHAT'S ONE AREA OF YOUR LIFE WHERE IT'S HARD TO BE WISE? WHAT'S ONE AREA WHERE YOU CONSTANTLY FIND YOURSELF WALKING RIGHT UP TO THE LINE?

Making the wise choice means listening to the small, sometimes quiet voice in your head. You know the one. The one that tugs at your heart and makes you sick to your stomach when you think about making a bad choice. It's there. It's *always* there. You just have to train yourself to listen.

WHETHER IT'S WHAT YOU SAY WITH YOUR MOUTH, WATCH WITH YOUR EYES, OR DO WITH YOUR BODY, WISDOM IS ALWAYS THE BEST BET.

That doesn't mean it's always easy. That doesn't mean it comes naturally. That doesn't mean you don't *really want that marshmallow*.

It means you are going to have to say some hard "no's" and some challenging "yes's." But it's in your best interest, to figure out how to do this. Why?

BECAUSE WISDOM SETS YOU UP TO LOVE YOUR LIFE.

WHAT WOULD IT MEAN TO CHOOSE WHAT'S WISE WHEN IT COMES TO THIS?

_____

_____

_____

_____

_____

· DAY FIVE ·
FOLLOW THROUGH

No one likes going to the doctor. Sure, you might get a lollipop (if you're lucky, and under age 10) but only after you've been poked and prodded and maybe even shot at (with needles, that is).

Yet, people still go to the doctor. Doctors' offices stay in business. Doctors' schedules stay full of poking and prodding day in and day out. Why??

Because being sick is worse than going to the doctor.

When you are sick, you are willing to do *anything* to feel better—including going to the doctor.

Think for a moment; what if you went to the doctor, got a prescription for medicine that would make you feel better, bought the medicine, took the medicine home, studied the medicine on the Internet, discovered how it interacts with the chemicals in your body, and even became such a fan of it that you decide to sell it for a living?

Would any of those things help you get better? No. Obviously. The only way medicine can help you is by *taking* it. Even if you fully and passionately believe in the medicine's ability to help you, it will never help you, unless you follow through and get it in your own system.

All of us know and understand that. No one is going to argue that just *believing* in the medicine, but not actually *taking* it, will make you healthy.

Yet, so often that's exactly what many of us do when it comes to God.

We believe what He says.

We know the right things to do.

We just don't follow through and actually *do* them.

Have you ever found yourself knowing what you should do, but not doing it? Maybe you lied even though you knew it was wrong. Maybe you ignored that feeling in your gut and gossiped about that kid in your class anyway. Maybe you needed a good grade so you justified cheating on a test. Or maybe it wasn't something you did *wrong*, it was just ignoring the *right* thing. Like noticing the sink piled high with dishes, but pretending not to see, so you wouldn't get stuck washing them all night.

It's probably happened more times than you would care to admit.

James, the brother of Jesus, talked about the importance of not just knowing the right thing to do, but following through and doing it. He said this:

> *Do not merely listen to the word, and so deceive yourselves.*
> *Do what it says.* (James 1:22)

What James is saying here could be a game-changer for how you live.

See, God's Word has many ideas about how to love your life and get the most out of your time on earth. Things like . . .

Be kind to others (Ephesians 4:22)

Pray for others (Matthew 5:44)

Love your enemies (Luke 6:27)

Tell the truth (Ephesians 4:25)

Be generous (1 Timothy 6:18)

Things a lot of us *know*. But knowing them isn't going to help your life; doing them will.

In other words, **if you know what to do, follow through.**

What James is basically saying in the passage is that unless you apply your faith, unless you move from thinking it's a good idea to *living* like it's a good idea, it doesn't have any real value to you.

Knowing this stuff in your head isn't doing you any favors. You need to actually *do* the things God is asking you to do.

Why? Because God wants to protect what's important to you. Your self-esteem, your relationships, your family, your future dating life, your future marriage. James is saying just because you may *believe* God's way is best doesn't mean you will love your life more. You have to apply what you believe for it to make a difference. So **if you know what to do, follow through.**

WHAT IS ONE AREA OF YOUR LIFE YOU AREN'T FOLLOWING THROUGH LIKE YOU KNOW YOU SHOULD?

_____

_____

_____

_____

WHAT IS STOPPING YOU?

_____

_____

_____

_____

WHAT MIGHT HAPPEN IF YOU CHOOSE TO FOLLOW THROUGH WITH WHAT YOU KNOW TO DO?

_____

_____

_____

_____

TRY THIS

When it comes to the Bible, it can feel like you are standing on the outside looking in. At times you find yourself thinking, *it sounds nice that God said and did all that for those people thousands of years ago, but what about me? What about now?*

Well, there's a way to read Scripture that makes you understand God's Word in a way you never have before. Check out the verses below. Then read them as if they are words directly from God to you. Fill in the blanks with **your name** and pay careful attention to what they say about *you*. Then spend some time thinking about what these verses say about *who* you are.

See what great love the Father has lavished on _____, that _____ should be called a child of God! And that is what _____ [is]! (1 John 3:1)

Many, O Lord my God, are the wonders you have done. The things you planned for _____ no one can recount to you; were I to speak and tell of them, they would be too many to declare. (Psalm 40:5)

. . . He [God] who began a good work in _____ will carry it on to completion until the day of Christ Jesus. (Philippians 1:6)

But now, God's message, the God who made you in the first place,
_____, the One who got you started, _____:
"Don't be afraid, I've redeemed you. I've called your name. You're
mine. When you're in over your head, I'll be there with you. When
you're in rough waters, you will not go down. When you're between
a rock and a hard place, it won't be a dead end—because I am God,
your personal God, the Holy of Israel, your Savior.
(Isaiah 43:1-3a, The Message)

"Never will I leave _____; never will I forsake
_____." (Hebrews 13:5b)

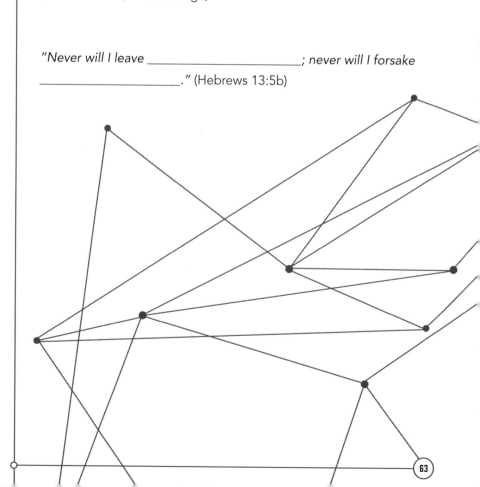

WEEK THREE
EMBRACE COMMUNITY

EMBRACE COMMUNITY

As a human, what are your basic needs? Oxygen, food, water, shelter, clothing. Anything else?

In 1943, a guy named Abraham Maslow made a pyramid of human needs and it actually had a lot more on it than you would think.[6] Sure, everyone needs food, water, and shelter to survive. Surprisingly, those only made up *one* of the five layers of Maslow's pyramid. He went on to prove that we don't just need the basics. We also need a sense of safety or security. And we all require relationships— people in our lives who make us feel like we fit, who offer us community, and give us a sense of belonging.

Think about it.

When you have a spare afternoon, seeing a movie with friends is better than going to see one alone.

When you ace that test you'd been stressing about, you want your family to know about it and celebrate the success.

When it feels like your world is falling apart, you want a friend to confide in.

When you have an impossible project to take on, working with people you like makes it more manageable.

When you're faced with a hard choice, you look to someone else for solid advice.

As a human, you *need* others.[7]

YOU ARE WIRED TO EMBRACE COMMUNITY.

All of those people you hang out with, get advice from, share a home with, play sports with, live near . . . that's your *community*.

But it's more than that, too. When we look back at what Jesus says in the book of Matthew about the Greatest Commandment, He tells us to love God and love others. The great thing about community is it allows us to do *both*. Because **you love God best when you love others**.

And when you . . .

> spend time with others,
>
> encourage others,
>
> learn from others,
>
> and resolve conflicts with others,

you may just be surprised how visible and close God becomes.

· DAY ONE ·
FRIENDS

Have you ever noticed how some dog owners resemble their dogs? If you haven't, take a couple minutes to Google "people who look like their dogs."

See? It's a real thing.

Scientists believe there's some unconscious thought process that causes us to pick our pet look-alike because of familiarity.[8] Sounds reasonable. Kind of.

While it's true dog owners sometimes look like their four-legged companions, it's also true people often look like the people they hang around, in both appearance and personality.[9]

In fact, studies show **you are the average of the five people you spend the most time around**.[10]

SO ... WHO ARE THE FIVE PEOPLE
YOU SPEND THE MOST TIME AROUND?

1.

2.

3.

4.

5.

IN WHAT WAYS DO YOU FIND
YOURSELF RESEMBLING THEM?

_____

_____

_____

_____

It makes sense. When you belong to a certain group of people socially, athletically, or academically, everyone sort of begins to dress the same, talk the same, and maybe even act the same.

That doesn't make you creepy. That makes you normal. Because **all of us, in some way or another, resemble those we hang around.**

King Solomon, a king of Israel during the most prosperous time in Israel's history, wrote about how we are affected by those we hang around. But Solomon was more than just a wealthy and influential king. He was, as we learned last week, also considered the wisest man to ever live besides Jesus. And this is what he says in the book of Proverbs:

> _Walk with the wise and become wise, for a companion_
> _of fools suffers harm._ (Proverbs 13:20)

So the wisest guy to have _ever_ lived tells us, "It doesn't matter how smart you are. If you hang out with fools, you get hurt."

How does he know?

It's not just because Solomon was super smart. He knew this because he experienced this principle firsthand. See, as wise as he was, Solomon ended up making some really bad choices . . . because of the people he hung out with.

Solomon had all the potential in the world, but being around the wrong kind of people led him down a painful path. It hurt his friendships. It hurt his reputation. It hurt his relationship with God.

Solomon learned the hard way that **your friends determine your direction**. The same is true for you.

It doesn't matter how smart you are.

It doesn't matter if you know the best thing to do.

It doesn't matter if you have a spotless track record.

When you hang out with foolish people, it hurts you. It trips you up. It keeps you from seeing the wise choices as clearly as you should.

HOW HAVE YOU SEEN "FOOLISH FRIENDSHIPS" HURT YOU OR THE PEOPLE AROUND YOU?

_____

_____

_____

Your friends determine your direction. No matter how independent, confident, or trendsetting you are, the people you hang around most have an effect on the choices you make. From where you hang out Friday night to how you treat others. From the teams you join to the classes you take. You are in a particular stage of life when your friends have a lot of power over the kind of person you become.

Choosing wise friends is essential for setting yourself up for the best possible future.

Friendship is awesome. God made friendship and wants you to embrace life with others—to share experiences with them. He wants you to connect with those who are going to help you become your best self and set you up for the most success. **God wants the best for you**, and good friends are part of that success.

So take a few minutes to think about your friends. Think about the five people whose names you listed at the beginning and the people you *choose* to hang around.

WRITE THREE THINGS YOU WANT TO BE TRUE ABOUT WHO YOU ARE AS A PERSON (SUCH AS KIND, THOUGHTFUL, FUNNY).

1.

2.

3.

ARE YOUR CURRENT FRIENDSHIPS HELPING YOU ACHIEVE THIS?

_____

WHAT DO YOU NEED TO CHANGE TO MAKE SURE THE FRIENDS YOU HAVE ARE HELPING YOU BECOME THE PERSON YOU WANT TO BE?

_____

_____

_____

· DAY TWO ·
BLIND SPOTS

We've all seen shapes in clouds. You look up and instead of seeing your typical white, puffy, cumulus cloud, you see a building, or a boat, or your best friend eating a burrito. It's really amazing the pictures your imagination can come up with.

But people don't just see shapes in clouds. They see images in all kinds of things.

Two baristas in Tennessee once thought they saw the face of Mother Teresa in a cinnamon bun. The coffee shop where it was discovered kept it on display for *ten years*.

Another woman from Miami swore she saw the face of Jesus in her grilled cheese sandwich. She later sold that grilled cheese for $28,000! Think about that before you start eating your next sandwich. It could be worth thousands of dollars!

It's amazing the complex things we can see when we look at stuff like clouds, cinnamon buns, and grilled cheese sandwiches. The truth is, we aren't nearly as aware when it comes to paying attention to our own lives.

ALL OF US HAVE A TENDENCY TO THINK WE ARE THE BEST EXPERTS WHEN IT COMES TO OUR OWN LIVES.

You know the best decisions for you. You like to decide for yourself where you go, who you go with, who your friends are, and who you date.

The problem is, you can't actually see yourself as well as you think. All of us are blind to things about ourselves that are obvious to everyone else. Maybe . . .

> you thought it would be fun to go to that party.

> you thought that person would make a great boyfriend or girlfriend.

> you thought those friends would always have your back.

But, turns out, you were wrong. You got in trouble. You got hurt. And you found yourself alone.

WHEN WAS THE LAST TIME YOU MADE A DECISION YOU THOUGHT WAS GOOD, BUT REGRETTED LATER? WHAT HAPPENED?

_____

_____

_____

_____

_____

_____

Everyone has blind spots. Especially when it comes to personal weaknesses. And if you don't know the areas you might need help, you are going to have trouble clearly seeing, and then making, the best decisions.

The book of Proverbs has a verse that offers a practical way for you to improve your blind spots. (King Solomon for the win. Again.)

> *The way of a fool is right in his own eyes,*
> *but a wise man listens to advice.* (Proverbs 12:15 ESV)

Solomon knew the problem: You can't always see yourself well enough to make the best decision. Sometimes you need advice from someone else, someone who can more clearly see your past or envision your future potential. Sometimes you need to listen to an outside voice more than you listen to your own. And God has put people in your life to be that voice of wisdom.

In other words, **to know the wise choice, find an outside voice**.

We are all masters of convincing ourselves we know best. You could easily convince yourself that eating chocolate fudge ice cream three times a day for the rest of your life is a wise choice. It wouldn't be hard at all to find a reason why you *need* to spend every penny you've been saving for a car on that concert ticket instead.

That's when you need an outside voice. That's when you need someone who cares enough about you to tell you the right decision, even if it makes you mad.

THAT'S WHEN YOU NEED TO FIND SOMEONE WHO CARES MORE ABOUT WHAT'S BEST FOR YOU THAN THEY CARE ABOUT YOU LIKING THEM.

Do you have a dating decision to make?

Find an outside voice.

Are you trying to figure out how to respond to your parents?

Find an outside voice.

Are you wondering if you should spend Friday night with that group of people?

Find an outside voice.

WHAT'S AN AREA IN WHICH YOU COULD
USE AN OUTSIDE VOICE RIGHT NOW?

_____

TO KNOW THE WISE CHOICE, FIND AN OUTSIDE VOICE.

WHO SHOULD YOUR OUTSIDE VOICE BE?
LIST A FEW PEOPLE YOU KNOW WHO CARE
MORE ABOUT WHAT'S BEST FOR YOU THAN
THEY DO ABOUT YOU LIKING THEM.

_____

_____

_____

_____

_____

· DAY THREE ·
ENCOURAGEMENT

Have you ever heard of Radical Honesty?

No, it's not an underground band or a hidden camera TV show. It's a small social movement introduced by a man named Brad Blanton. The idea behind "Radical Honesty" is for people to have closer relationships with one another by being totally honest . . . all the time.[11]

That means you never consider the other person's feelings, but just say exactly what you think, *no filter.*

> "Your outfit is terrible."

> "Your breath is awful."

> "Your nose is *huge.*"

It's easy to see why it's only a *small* movement.

Most people know that kind of honesty would be tough for relationships to survive. Why? Because voicing every negative thought we have is a sure friendship-killer.

The biggest problem with hearing negative comments is they tend to stick.

WHAT NEGATIVE MESSAGE HAVE YOU HEARD AT SOME POINT THAT HAS STUCK WITH YOU? HOW HAS IT AFFECTED THE WAY YOU SEE YOURSELF?

_____

_____

_____

_____

Studies have shown if you hear one negative comment, you need five positive ones to combat it.[12]

For every . . .

"You're really not that great at math, are you?"

You need five . . .

"You're a great friend."

"Thank you for saving me a seat."

"I could tell you worked really hard at practice today."

"I love that you're someone I can count on."

"I appreciate your help after school."

NEGATIVE COMMENTS ARE STRONG, BUT WHEN USED OFTEN ENOUGH, POSITIVE COMMENTS CAN BE _STRONGER._

This idea isn't new.

The apostle Paul, the guy responsible for writing most of the New Testament, sent a letter to one of the churches he started, communicating the same idea. In this letter he writes,

> _Therefore encourage one another and build each other up,_
> _just as in fact you are doing._ (1 Thessalonians 5:11)

During this time period in the Roman Empire, Christianity wasn't exactly a popular religion or lifestyle choice. Jesus followers worried about their future—like whether they would be arrested or even killed for what they believed. In other words, life was stressful.

The great thing is that the believers at Thessalonica didn't use their stress as an excuse to cut each other down (and let's be honest, going negative is especially easy when we're stressed.) Instead, they dealt with their dangerous situation by using positive words and uplifting messages.

Paul got word of their behavior and tells them to keep it up! He reminds them, in a time when it would be much easier to talk negatively, the positive has even more power.

To encourage others, just like Paul did, we need to replace the negativity with positive thoughts. Try not only to *think* positive thoughts about others, but *say them.*

Paul is telling you, **don't keep your (nice) thoughts to yourself**.

Paul not only knew it was second nature to think negatively, but also knew not all of us are great at actually saying the good stuff we think. We assume, *she probably gets compliments all the time.* Or, *his head is already too big.* Or, *I'll sound like a weirdo if I point out something like that.*

The truth is, everyone is struggling to outweigh the negative messages with positive ones. It doesn't matter if that guy in your class has heard he's brilliant four times today. Someone just called him a freak and he might just need that fifth encouragement to combat the one insult. Remember,

DON'T KEEP YOUR NICE THOUGHTS TO YOURSELF.

Because when you get down to it, it's not just about boosting someone's self-esteem. It's about the Greatest Commandment—about loving others.

WHAT IS ONE POSITIVE MESSAGE YOU
REMEMBER HEARING? HOW DID IT
AFFECT THE WAY YOU SEE YOURSELF?

_____

_____

_____

What if instead of radical honesty, you practiced radical positivity? Send that text. Make the call. Have a conversation. **Don't keep your (nice) thoughts to yourself!**

WHO CAN YOU ENCOURAGE TODAY? HOW
CAN YOU ENCOURAGE THAT PERSON?

_____

_____

FEELING SUPER INSPIRED? MAKE A LIST OF FOUR OR
MORE PEOPLE YOU CAN ENCOURAGE THIS WEEK OR IN
THE WEEKS TO COME, THEN GET STARTED. DECIDE TO:

_____ **MAKE A PLAN.**

_____ **PICK YOUR WORDS.**

_____ **PICK YOUR DEVICE**
                            (phone, text, email).

_____ **THEN DO IT.**

· DAY FOUR ·
CONFLICT

What do you think is the longest-running show on television?

Nope, not a sports program. Not a news program. Not even a reality show.

A daytime drama called *Guiding Light* has the Guinness World Record for being the longest-running show on American television. In fact, it *pre-dates* television. It started on the radio in 1937, before TVs were even common.[13]

While soap operas have a bad reputation for having ridiculous plots, when you've been around for eighty years and filmed over 15,000 television episodes, you have to get creative about the stories you tell.

Guiding Light has definitely gotten "creative."

When character Reva Lewis was cloned from one of her own frozen cells (let's pause to let that first part sink in . . .), she found her clone to be evil and with a secret agenda all her own. Most people would think a storyline like that is completely ridiculous . . .and they would be right. So how do soap operas manage to stay around so long? They have one important element:

Conflict.

Every soap opera, every reality TV show, every drama, every famous book, or movie saga has conflict. Conflict is entertaining.

We all love to see a struggle and how it's going to be resolved. Without it, we get bored and lose interest in a story.

Conflict in movies and in soap operas is one thing, but conflict when it comes to real life is something completely different.

WHEN YOU LIVE IN COMMUNITY, YOU WILL FACE CONFLICT. AND HOW YOU HANDLE THAT CONFLICT DETERMINES THE QUALITY OF YOUR COMMUNITY.

Conflict in relationships brings frustration, anger, and pain. We hate dealing with it. So we ignore it. We pretend it doesn't exist. We may try to avoid the person like last week's mystery meat in the school cafeteria.

Ignoring conflict doesn't really work though, does it? Just because you find a way to *appear* like everything is fine, conflict has a tendency to make you *feel* anything but fine. In other words, even though you may try, **you can't escape conflict**.

James, in the book with his name on it, talks about conflict saying,

What causes fights and quarrels among you? Don't they come from your desires that battle within you? You desire but do not have, so you kill. You covet but you cannot get what you want, so you quarrel and fight. You do not have because you do not ask God.
(James 4:1-2)

James isn't afraid to step on anyone's toes. "What causes conflict?" he asks. You. No sugarcoating about it. (Apparently James was a follower of the Radical Honesty movement before it ever became popular.)

James knows **you are the secret to resolving and dealing with conflict**. You can't control someone else. So to deal with conflict you have to be able to turn your focus from *what they did* to *what you can do to make it better.*

THE FIRST STEP TO HANDLING CONFLICT IS PAYING ATTENTION TO THE PART YOU PLAYED IN IT.

The sooner you can see what you've done to create the conflict, the sooner you can start doing what needs to be done to fix it.

And fixing it is the goal.

Even if it feels uncomfortable.

Even if it makes you cringe at the thought of it.

Even if you have to admit you are wrong in the process (and you will).

Even if it feels like the other person is getting away with it (and it will).

The faster you own it, the faster you can fix it and the easier it becomes to **resolve it now, not later**.

This is important because **the longer you put conflict off, the harder it becomes to fix**, the more complicated it becomes, the more emotions get involved, and the more opportunity for things to be said and heard (and texted) the wrong way.

But when you make the decision to **resolve it now, not later**, you are doing more than solving a problem, you are potentially saving a relationship.

No matter the wrongdoing—from a stolen eraser to an evil cloned twin—make the decision today to make things right. Even if it isn't totally fixed, do your part to make peace.

WHAT IS ONE RELATIONSHIP THAT COULD USE
A CONFLICT FIX? WHAT CAN YOU DO TODAY
TO MAKE STEPS TOWARDS RESOLUTION?

_____

_____

_____

_____

_____

_____

CHECK OUT THE "TRY THIS" ON PAGE 88 FOR
SOME POINTERS ON HOW TO RESOLVE
THE CONFLICT THAT NEEDS FIXING.

· DAY FIVE ·
A SAFE PLACE

A few years ago, a woman named Lisa Rogak wrote a book, *One Big Happy Family*, about animals that became replacement parents for an orphaned animal of another species.

There's the story of the family of cats "adopting" a baby squirrel.

The dog who protected a bullied monkey at a zoo in China.

And Edgar Alan Pig stepping in to father a one-week-old lamb.

Why do people love these stories so much?

Because they are so **unexpected**. These stories wouldn't be nearly as interesting if a dog was taking care of a puppy or a pig had adopted a piglet. These stories are unusual because we all tend to stick with those who are like us.

We like people who dress like us, like the same kind of music we do, enjoy the same kind of movies and play the same sports. It's easier that way, isn't it?

WHAT ARE SOME OF THE THINGS YOU HAVE
IN COMMON WITH THE GROUP OF PEOPLE
YOU HANG OUT WITH?

_____

_____

_____

It's not bad. It's human nature.

It only becomes a problem when we allow differences to create distance and separate us from others.

Community is complicated for a lot of reasons. But community is also really great. The tricky thing about it—what makes it hard—is the same thing that makes it awesome. Community would be boring if everyone was the same. It would be like going to Cold Stone Creamery and always getting vanilla ice cream when there are so many other options, other flavors, other toppings, other cones!

YOU CAN'T EXPERIENCE THE BEST OF COMMUNITY WHEN EVERYONE AROUND YOU IS EXACTLY LIKE YOU.

Doing life with people who aren't like you is *complicated*. (You already know this. You live with your family—and that's no joke.) When you do life with people who are different from you, you have to work harder to connect.

> You have to be patient sharing a room with someone who hates the music you love.

> You have to get creative when someone you're close with doesn't communicate like you do.

> You have to make decisions every single day to make sure your most important relationships stay healthy.

In the New Testament, the apostle Paul gives us great advice about community in his letter to the Ephesians. Paul writes,

> *Be completely humble and gentle; be patient,*
> *bearing with one another in love.* (Ephesians 4:2)

What makes this passage even better is that Paul was in prison for telling people about Jesus when he wrote it. Paul was alone. He wasn't getting to experience community so he wanted to make sure those who were experiencing community did it right.

Paul knew community is hard. But he also knew it's better than being alone. He knew it's worth fighting for and worth doing well. Which is why Paul urges the Ephesians—and you—to be humble, gentle, patient, and full of love—even with those who are different from you. Especially with those different from you. And the best way to experience community with people who aren't exactly like you is to **be a safe place**.

Being a safe place means other people can trust you to not gossip about them, not make them feel or look dumb, not use their weaknesses to make you look better—even when they don't have it all together.

Being a safe place means you are . . .

humble enough to let others get the credit.

kind when it's easier to get revenge.

patient enough not to make others look stupid when they don't understand.

loving even when you have a hard time finding something in common.

accepting of differences even when they make you uncomfortable.

BE A SAFE PLACE.

For everyone.

For your little sister who has one tone of voice: whining.

For your science partner who hasn't discovered the benefits of deodorant.

For your parents whose arguments shake the walls of your house.

For the person you don't understand, can't see eye-to-eye with, and would rather pretend doesn't exist.

Community is only as good as you are willing to make it. When you make the decision to be humble, gentle, patient, and loving, you're likely to have more *real* friendships. You're likely to have relationships in which you feel safe to be your real self at all times.

So decide to **be a safe place.**

Because when you are, you don't just make yourself look good, you make *God* look good. Because He is the ultimate safe place for you and for the people around you.

WHO IS ONE PERSON IN YOUR EVERYDAY LIFE YOU DON'T HAVE MUCH IN COMMON WITH?

_____

WHAT ARE SOME WAYS YOU COULD BE A SAFE PLACE FOR THAT PERSON?

_____

_____

_____

_____

TRY THIS

Community with others is one of the best things God has given us. Unfortunately, conflict that isn't handled or dealt with is one of the fastest ways to hurt a healthy community. While it isn't *always* something we can control, more often than not, our conflict is partly a result of actions we *could have controlled.*

So . . . **what do you do about conflict you helped create?**

Below, you'll find a guide for how to get to the root of the problem, how to talk through it and where to go from here. Owning your part in a conflict can be tough, but when you get to the other side, you'll be so glad you did.

One of the best ways to end a battle is to apologize for the part of the conflict you created. But sometimes it's hard to know what to say and how to say it. Use the questions below to think through how to begin a conversation with someone you need to apologize to.

WHO IS SOMEONE I NEED TO APOLOGIZE TO?

_____

Think about what you are apologizing for. Be specific. The more specific you are in an apology, the more the other person will know you mean it. Ask yourself the following questions:

MY ACTIONS. What did you do? _____

_____

MY WORDS. What did you say?_____

_____

MY TONE. How did you say it?_____

MY ATTITUDE. How did you show it?_____

_____

How do you think it made the other person feel?_____

_____

What is one way you could respond better next time?_____

_____

Now use this guide to write out your apology. After you write it, decide whether you want to text it to them, write it out and hand it to them, or say it to them in person.

Dear _____ **,**

I am very sorry that I

_____ .

I realize it was wrong because

_____ .

and there's a good chance it made you feel

_____ .

It's very important to me to get this right. So next time I'll do

my best to_____ .

Please forgive me.

Sincerely,

_____

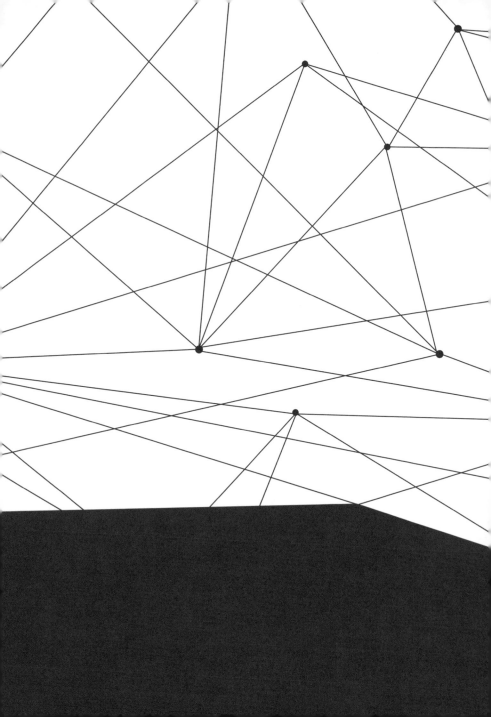

WEEK FOUR
SERVE OTHERS

SERVE OTHERS

Most of us love the idea of helping others.

You hear of someone who has a need and you think to yourself, "*I want to do something about that.*" Or, "*I hope they get the help they need and things turn around.*"

But a lot of times, when it comes to putting an actual plan into action, you just don't do it.

> You've got places to go.
>
> People to hang out with.
>
> Netflix to binge on.

It's hard to rearrange your schedule. It's inconvenient to go above and beyond. Maybe you aren't even sure *what* you would do if you had the chance to help.

It's easy to stay in your same old pattern or "comfort zone," leaving the serving up to someone else and thinking someone else will take care of it. Someone else will know what to do.

But a unique thing happens when you make a plan to help someone and then decide to go through with it. **You hardly remember what was asked of you. Instead, you remember what it did for others.**

You discover what it feels like . . .

> to use what you have for something bigger.
>
> to work alongside others to accomplish something you couldn't have done alone.

to actually do the things you believe matter, instead of standing by while someone else does the work.

The best part is, what you do lets someone else know they really matter—to you and to God.

YOU ARE WIRED TO SERVE OTHERS.

Every time you serve and help others, you are doing more than just fulfilling God's Greatest Commandment to love Him and love others. **You are participating in the story you are wired to join—a story bigger than you could imagine.**

· DAY ONE ·
COMPASSION

What one word would you use to describe . . .

STAR WARS? _____

REALITY TV? _____

AMUSEMENT PARKS? _____

YOUR GRANDMA? _____

SKYDIVING? _____

GIRLS? _____

BOYS? _____

FRENCH FRIES? _____

YOUR BEST FRIEND? _____

Have you ever heard of the game show called *Password*? Two teams compete against each other to guess a random word (the "password"). One person is secretly given the "password" and has to come up with a one-word clue to give the other teammate in hopes it is enough to guess the right word. If the word isn't guessed after just one clue, the next team has a chance to guess.

Talk about high pressure. How can you describe "caterpillar" or "nachos" in just *one word*?

Now imagine having to come up with *one* word to describe . . .*God*. Remember trying to think of words to describe God in week one?

(Feels like forever ago, right?) It was hard enough to narrow Him down to three words, but ONE? It seems practically impossible. God is complicated.

A 13th-century theologian (someone whose job was to study and learn about God) decided to give it a try. He said, "**You may call God love; you may call God goodness; but the best name for God is compassion.**"[14]

HOW WOULD YOU DESCRIBE COMPASSION? (FEEL FREE TO USE MORE THAN ONE WORD)

_____

_____

_____

_____

In the gospels, Jesus (who is the physical representation of God) is described as having compassion _twelve different times_. In one of those places, Matthew 9:36, the scene is described this way,

When He saw the crowds, He had compassion on them, because they were harassed and helpless, like sheep without a shepherd.

So what is compassion exactly? **Compassion is noticing somebody's difficult situation—and doing something about it.**

Just like this verse suggests, everywhere Jesus went, the crowds would follow. Who could blame them? Jesus, from the very beginning, caught people's attention in the most unusual ways.

He healed people's diseases.

He cured lifelong deformities.

He spoke with an understanding of God that stunned those listening.

So everywhere Jesus went, the crowds followed.

They followed Him to see the latest and greatest miracle He would perform—and most of the time, Jesus did not disappoint. But Jesus didn't perform miracles like a one-man circus act complete with a loud "TA-DA!" at the end. He didn't take a bow, sign autographs, and ask for tips after each one.

JESUS HAD A MOTIVE THAT DROVE HIM TO HELP PEOPLE: COMPASSION.

The word compassion literally means "to suffer with," which is exactly what Jesus did. He didn't just notice people's misfortune; He suffered *with them*. His goal wasn't to simply fix their problems, but to see people as individuals to care for, instead of problems to solve.

And Jesus asks you to do the same. Sure, Jesus had some advantages you don't have. You probably haven't quite mastered the whole miracle thing. But, it was more than Jesus' ability to heal that made Him compassionate. It was His ability to *pay attention* to others.

This is one way—one BIG way—we get to be like Jesus. You are wired to serve others. And serving begins with noticing. Noticing a need. Noticing a person. **Then deciding to care about that person**.

Sure, we need to care about the problem, but we need to care about the *person* with the problem *more*. That's what Jesus did. That's how Jesus showed compassion.

HOW DOES COMPASSION FOR A PERSON LOOK DIFFERENT THAN SIMPLY WANTING TO FIX A PROBLEM?

_____

_____

Jesus saw more than a body needing help. He saw people sick with loneliness and heartache. He saw people broken from hurt and insecurity. He saw people ill with fear and uncertainty. He **decided to care** and then to *do* something because He cared. You don't have to be God's Son to do the same.

You can also see a need and do your part to fix it. You can see a problem and a person and **decide to care**. Maybe it's something super practical like a new pair of shoes or a warm meal. Or maybe it's simply showing up when someone is down.

You can be a friend.

You can offer encouragement.

You can listen.

You can give your time.

WHAT IS ONE WAY YOU CAN SERVE OTHERS WITH COMPASSION? WHAT IS ONE THING YOU WILL DO FOR THEM?

_____

_____

_____

· DAY TWO ·
PURPOSE

Did you know that . . .

> a hippo's body creates its own sunscreen?
>
> cockroaches can live for weeks without a head?
>
> frogs can see 360 degrees around them?
>
> crocodiles swallow stones to balance them in the water and help them digest their food?[15]

God has quite the imagination. There are no limits to the things His creation can do. But God didn't just make these animals this way for fun. God created them exactly as they are for a *reason*.

Hippos live on the hottest continent on Earth. So sweat that doubles as sunscreen is a pretty sweet deal.

Frogs fall pretty low on the food chain; they're the perfect snack for more than a few animals. So it's a great advantage to have eyes that can do a 360 and keep them out of danger.

The things that seem strange or maybe just a "fun fact" to us are the things that God *intentionally* wired into animals for a purpose.

Now think about this: The same intentionality God used for designing animals, He used when designing *you*. In fact, God got really creative when it came to making every single part of your personality and temperament. Not just for fun, but because **behind every part of your wiring God has a *purpose***. He gave you certain gifts, abilities, and talents—not just for a cool party trick, but for a much bigger reason. And it's up to you to discover who you were made to be and what to do to make the most of who you are.

God specifically wired everyone—yes, *everyone*—to excel in certain things.

WHAT ARE A FEW THINGS ABOUT YOU THAT MAKE YOU UNIQUE . . . A TALENT, AN INTEREST, AN EVENT IN YOUR LIFE, ETC.?

_____

_____

_____

_____

_____

Maybe you're great at playing basketball. Or maybe you're a chess champ.

Maybe you're a fantastic listener. Or maybe you can keep a crowd of people entertained for hours.

Maybe you handle details and deadlines really well. Or maybe you're super creative and can make any space feel inviting, comfortable and cool.

Maybe you love to cook. Or maybe you love to clean.

Maybe you're great at fixing stuff. Or maybe you're good at assembling furniture from IKEA.

Whatever it is, you are *wired* that way. God made you that way on purpose. What's even better is that **who God has wired you to be reveals what God has made you to *do***.

You may read that and panic. *How do I make a living putting together Swedish furniture?!?!*

Good news. Your wiring doesn't have to determine your career. Your wiring determines your *gifts*—the stuff God gave you that makes you, *you*. And those gifts can be used in any area of your life, at any age and in a ton of different ways. Not just so you can *make a living* and earn a salary from them, but so you can *make a life* and find purpose in them.

In a letter to the church in Ephesus, the apostle Paul writes,

For we are God's workmanship, created in Christ Jesus to do good works, which God prepared in advance for us to do. (Ephesians 2:10)

GOD HAS DONE WORK IN YOU SO THAT YOU MIGHT DO GOOD WORK IN THE WORLD AROUND YOU.

In other words, it's important to discover how God wired you so you can use your unique gifts to serve others.

God designed both who you would *be* and what you would *do* when He made you. He gave you specific gifts because He had a dream for how you would use them. Not to put pressure on you, but He did this in hopes that you would dream big and **serve others in a big way.**

You get to decide how to use the gifts that are wired into you. Great news, you can start today. In fact, you can start right now.

WHAT CAN YOU DO WITH YOUR GIFTS TODAY TO HELP SOMEONE IN THE WORLD AROUND YOU?

_____

_____

_____

_____

_____

· DAY THREE ·
TEAMWORK

Think about how it feels when you hear snow is in the forecast. The meteorologist is certain four to six inches will fall overnight. You have visions of sledding down the huge hill in your neighborhood, making snow angels, and avoiding yellow snow at all costs. The best part? School might be canceled!

Or . . . will it?

Because let's be honest, when the snow starts, it hardly ever looks like it will amount to anything. A few stray flakes land on your mom's windshield and you think, "This is a total sham! There's no way this will add up to school being canceled!"

Have you ever thought of yourself as being like a snowflake? Okay, probably not. Or at least not since your Kindergarten teacher said, *We're all unique little snowflakes.* But have you ever felt as completely *insignificant* as one single snowflake seems? You see all these big problems in your neighborhood, city, and world and think, **"How could anything I do really make a difference?"**

In some ways, you're right (not to be a downer). The world has big problems that need big solutions. One person isn't going to fix everything. But don't count yourself out. A snowflake by itself isn't much to talk about, but a whole bunch of snow is a different story! When a bunch of small and seemingly worthless snow flakes fall *together* and they just keep falling, they have the power to shut down an entire city.

SO, IMAGINE WHAT'S POSSIBLE WHEN WE WORK TOGETHER.

Together,

> we could change a lot of lives.
>
> we could change an entire school.
>
> we could change a whole city.
>
> we could change the world.

It might sound silly, but it's true. Together, we *can* do *more* than we could have done on our own.

WHEN WAS THE LAST TIME YOU WORKED WITH A TEAM OF PEOPLE TO ACCOMPLISH SOMETHING BIG?

_____

_____

WHAT DID YOU LIKE ABOUT WORKING AS A TEAM?

_____

_____

God created and called you to make a difference. He knows that's a big task, which is why He didn't design you to do it alone.

The apostle Paul used the idea of a body to help his readers understand how they were supposed to work together.

In fact, God has placed the parts in the body, every one of them, just as He wanted them to be. If they were all one part, where would the body be? As it is, there are many parts, but one body.
(1 Corinthians 12:18-20)

Like a hand, foot, or eye, each one of us has something to do that matters to the whole operation. You were never wired to exist on your own. Aside from the fact that an eyeball all by itself is creepy, it's also a lot less effective than when it's connected with every other body part. When it goes where it belongs and when it partners with the rest of the body, big things happen. The same is true for you. Your friends. Your small group. The people at your church. They can all work together like one body. Just like each part of a body works together to do more than one foot could all by itself, **together we can do more**.

You can't do everything. You aren't *supposed* to. When it comes to serving, you have to do more than just *know* what you're good at. You need to make an effort to partner with others and rely on them to do what you *weren't* wired to do. Only then will the *magic* happen.

On your own you're small. You're limited. You're unable to fix the world's biggest problems. But, when each of us works collectively, we can make a huge difference in big and overwhelming issues like hunger, or poverty, or homelessness, or supplying clean water.

Imagine what serving others would look like if we all considered ourselves part of something much bigger than just our own gifts and talents? Because alone, you may feel insignificant, but **together we can do more**.

WHAT PROBLEMS IN THE WORLD BOTHER YOU MOST?

_____

_____

_____

WHAT CAN YOU BEGIN TO DO ABOUT THEM?

_____

_____

WHO COULD YOU ASK TO HELP YOU?

_____

_____

Here are some global organizations you could join with to help:

Compassion.org   CharityWater.org   RestavekFreedom.org

But you don't have to think outside your country or even your neighborhood to notice problems you could help to solve.

There are people right under your own roof you can practice this idea with. You already know how different you are from your family. Now imagine if you used those differences, the things each of you excel in, to accomplish something really good (instead of just getting on each other's nerves all the time).

BRAINSTORM SOME WAYS ALL OF YOU COULD DO SOMETHING TOGETHER TO ACCOMPLISH MORE THAN WHAT YOU COULD ON YOUR OWN.

_____

_____

_____

NOW PITCH SOME OF YOUR IDEAS TO YOUR FAMILY AND MAKE A PLAN FOR WHO TO HELP AND HOW TO HELP—_TOGETHER._

· DAY FOUR ·
THE INSIDE

February 14 is known as a day of love. It's also known as a day for eating boxes and boxes of chocolates. Americans spend nearly $345 million buying roughly 58 million pounds of chocolate during the week of Valentine's Day.

We might have a problem.

Who can blame us? Chocolate is *the best*. Still, there is one HUGE frustration with those ridiculous heart-shaped boxes of chocolate. You can never tell what's *inside*! Nothing is worse than choosing a delicious-looking chocolate only to bite into it and find lemon cream or an almond or whatever you don't like. So to help you out, here's a quick guide:

Caramels are usually square.

Chocolates that are round have soft centers, such as truffles or whips.

Rectangular candies are usually filled with nougat.

Oval candies most often contain butter fudge.[16]

It turns out the secret to knowing what's inside is all in the shape. You're welcome.

Wouldn't it be nice if you had a similar guide to know what was on the inside of a person? If you could tell if someone was really genuine or a fake? If you could really tell what the heart of a person was?

Good news! There is.

The way someone behaves is the best guide to seeing what's important to a person. Many times, people's outward actions give you clues into what they really believe and what they really care about.

Sounds great, right? But be careful, because what's true for others is also true for you.

YOUR ACTIONS TELL PEOPLE WHAT MATTERS MOST TO YOU.

It's important to care about serving your community and making it a better place. But the only way for people to know that stuff matters to you is if you *do* something about it.

WHAT DO YOU THINK ARE THE BIGGEST NEEDS IN YOUR COMMUNITY?

_____

_____

James says something huge about the idea of helping those in need:

Religion that God our Father accepts as pure and faultless is this: to look after orphans and widows in their distress and to keep oneself from being polluted by the world. (James 1:27)

James is saying, "You want to know what God cares about? You want to know the religion God is most interested in? It isn't that you know all the right facts or go to church a certain number of times a week or carry your Bible around in the halls of your school. **God cares about what you *do* to help others.**"

In other words, **the way you serve on the outside shows what you believe on the inside**.

The good news about this is that everyone can do something. All of us have the ability and the potential to see a need and meet that need. Maybe you discovered your community has more hungry people than you realized. Maybe you noticed there are a lot of kids who are struggling in school. Maybe you saw there are a lot of senior citizens who are lonely and could use some company. You can do something about every need you discover. You can . . .

organize a food drive.

serve monthly at your local food shelter.

offer tutoring classes.

be part of a reading program for kids.

start or join an adopt-a-grandparent program.

There are so many ways you can make what you believe on the inside visible on the outside. You just need to **decide how to serve—*and then do it.*** Simply take action.

LET THE WAY YOU SERVE ON THE OUTSIDE SHOW WHAT YOU BELIEVE ON THE INSIDE.

Just like the shape of a chocolate lets us know what's inside, the shape of your life lets the world know what's inside of you.

REMEMBER SOME OF THE NEEDS YOU THOUGHT OF ON PAGE 107? WHAT'S *ONE* YOU ARE INTERESTED IN HELPING WITH?

_____

_____

_____

WHAT IS ONE STEP YOU CAN TAKE THIS WEEK TO HELP A PERSON IN NEED, OR A CAUSE IN YOUR COMMUNITY?

_____

_____

_____

· DAY FIVE ·
GOD'S STORY

Have you ever seen a flash mob before? The definition of a flash mob is *a group of people who gather in a public place to do an unusual and pointless act.*

The first flash mob took place at a Macy's department store when a group of almost 150 people stood around an expensive rug. That's right. They just stood there. Not very exciting.[17]

Flash mobs have gotten way cooler. Now they include choreographed dance moves and sing-alongs. Now the people watching smile, clap, and think to themselves, "What I would give to be a part of that."

WHAT IS ONE THING YOU HAVE SEEN THAT MADE YOU WISH YOU COULD JOIN IN?

_____

_____

WHAT MADE YOU WANT TO BE A PART OF IT?

_____

_____

In some ways, God's story is like a flash mob.

Sometimes it's unfolding all around us and we don't even realize it. Other times we're lucky enough to see big pieces of it come together—

pieces that surprise us and wow us. But what makes it better than any flash mob in history is that when we see God's story, we don't have to just sit back and be observers. We don't have to stay on the sidelines and wish there was room for us.

We have the chance to *get involved*.

In the last meal with His followers, we get an idea of who Jesus wants us to be.

I no longer call you servants, because a servant does not know his master's business. Instead, I have called you friends, for everything that I learned from my Father I have made known to you. You did not choose me, but I chose you and appointed you to go and bear fruit—fruit that will last. (John 15:15-16a)

HOW WOULD THINKING OF YOURSELF AS JESUS' FRIEND CHANGE THE WAY YOU TALK TO HIM?

_____

_____

HOW COULD IT CHANGE THE WAY YOU THINK ABOUT HIM?

_____

_____

Jesus has big plans for His followers to participate in the work He is doing in the world. To **step into God's story**. You aren't kept out of the loop. You aren't left standing around wondering how something so amazing is happening around you and feeling like you missed the chance to participate.

You are a friend invited to join God in doing something bigger in the world.

You get to play a part in the story the God of the universe is writing.

You get to have a role in the work God is doing to draw people to Himself, to make old things new, make wrong things right, and make broken things whole.

YOU GET TO STEP INTO GOD'S STORY.

And when you do, you get the privilege of being called a *friend* of Jesus.

So, do you want to be part of something BIGGER than you? **Maybe it's time to step off the sidelines for good.**

How? Start exactly where you are. Consider becoming more involved in God's story . . .

in the way you interact with your family—with patience.

in the way you treat your friends—with kindness.

in the way you talk about your enemies—with compassion.

in the way you handle your time—with intention.

in the way you use your money—with wisdom.

in the way you get into relationships—and the way you get out of them—with honor.

You are surrounded with opportunities *every single day* . . .

TO CONNECT WITH GOD.

TO LOVE YOUR LIFE.

TO EMBRACE COMMUNITY.

TO SERVE OTHERS.

Every time you do these things, you are choosing to play your part in a bigger story. God's story.

It may be the end of this book, but this could be the start of something really great. Because **God's story is *bigger* than yours could ever be on its own**. When you participate, it makes your story **better** than it could have ever been apart from His.

You'll never regret making the decision to wrap your life into the story God is telling. After all, it's what you are *wired* to do.

WHAT'S ONE WAY YOU CAN STEP INTO GOD'S STORY TODAY?

_____

_____

STILL A LITTLE UNSURE ABOUT WHAT BEING IN GOD'S STORY MEANS FOR YOU? CHECK OUT THE <u>WHAT'S NEXT</u> SECTION ON PAGE 116 FOR WHAT MIGHT BE YOUR NEXT STEP.

TRY THIS

So, how exactly has God wired you? Chances are, this isn't something you've spent a lot of time trying to figure out until now. And chances are you won't discover everything about yourself in the next few minutes (or weeks or years). But let's start with a few questions.

WHAT DO YOU THINK YOU ARE GOOD AT?
(This can be anything. It doesn't have to be something that fits in a "religious" category. Simply think about what comes easily to you and doesn't come easily to everyone else.)

_____

_____

_____

WHAT'S IMPORTANT TO YOU?
(In other words, what things get you fired up? What do you love? What is something you can't stop thinking about?)

_____

_____

_____

WHAT DO YOU HAVE MORE OF THAN YOU NEED? WHAT ARE SOME THINGS YOU CAN GIVE AWAY?
(Think about something other than money—although money could be something, too. It could be time, stuff or even a skill.)

_____

_____

Next, take this list and your answers to a few different people—maybe your parents, your small group leader or student pastor, a coach, or club sponsor, maybe even a friend that you trust.

Ask them how they would answer these questions about you. You may be surprised how they see something you're really good at that you never noticed before. Or something you have never considered that important as one of your deepest passions.

Once you and those who know you best have answered these questions about you, **make a plan**.

Use the answers you've gathered to decide how to use your unique wiring to serve others.

Then . . . **make it happen**.

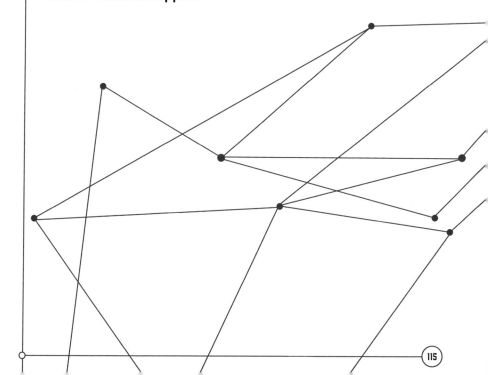

WHAT'S NEXT?

You're pretty bummed this awesome book is over, aren't you?

You had a great time laughing, crying and wishing it would never end. But it did. You got to the end of the fourth week and feel like you are off to a great start learning how you are wired and how the world, God, and others are all wired. And now you are off to master another of life's biggest mysteries.

OR . . .

maybe you finished week four and still have a lot of questions. Maybe you were left wondering, what's next? You've read about becoming a participant in God's story. You've started practicing some of the ideas you found earlier in the book. But maybe you don't feel like you are in the story like you want to be. Maybe you feel like you're doing all the right things but still wondering *why* you're doing them.

It could be, that you *are* missing something—an actual ***relationship with God***.

Let's break those three words down a little.

The good news:

GOD LOVES YOU.

It's important to start there. Because who wants to have a relationship with someone who is still trying to decide if they even like you? But with God, there's no question. Before He ever asked you to love Him, He first made His love for *you* very obvious. He made you. He fought for you. He loves you.

The bad news:

WE'RE ALL BROKEN.

Chances are you know this already. You know when you *don't* do the things you know you *should* do. You know when you hold on to a grudge for a little too long. When you twist your story a bit so you can get off the hook with your parents. When you talk badly about people behind their backs.

We're broken because we do things we know aren't right. And in the process we hurt others and we hurt ourselves.

That's sin.

THE MORE WE SIN, THE HARDER IT IS TO MAKE WISE CHOICES.

Sin keeps you from seeing what's true about God, yourself, and others. Sin makes you think you know best about what to do and that God is somehow against you. **Sin keeps you trapped in bad behavior and bad thinking.**

But worst of all, sin creates distance between you and God.

Sin can make you hide from God because you think He wants to punish you. But God isn't interested in disciplining your sin just to teach you a lesson and He isn't out to catch you.

That's because **God is the perfect Father**. As a perfect dad, He cares most about making the relationship between you and Him right. He knows sin has its own consequences. He isn't interested in punishing you more. God *is* interested in *freeing* you for something better and closing the gap sin created in His relationship with you.

How?

By sending Jesus. God sent His Son to live on Earth and experience life with you—to show you how strong God's affection is for you. And when Jesus died, He made right what sin broke in your relationship with God. Where sin separated you from God, Jesus' love brought you close again.

JESUS' DEATH SENT THE MESSAGE THAT NO SIN COULD CHANGE THE WAY GOD FEELS ABOUT YOU.

It gets even better.

Three days after Jesus was crucified and killed, God actually *raised Jesus from the dead*. Talk about extreme power. God showed that His love, demonstrated through Jesus, was bigger than any obstacle your sin could create—that His love could close the biggest distance. Because of Jesus' death and His resurrection, nothing—not sin and not even death—has the power to keep you from God's love.

So . . . what's next?

Because God sent Jesus, because of what Jesus did on the cross, because Jesus rose from the dead, you have the opportunity to have a close relationship with God. You have the opportunity to trust in what Jesus did but also to trust in Jesus Himself. You have the opportunity to trust that . . .

Jesus is who He says He is—God's Son.

God is who He says He is—a perfect heavenly Father.

God's biggest desires for your life are that you know He loves you, He is for you, He wants what's best for you, and He wants to be in a healthy relationship with you.

If you decide you trust and believe in all those things, you've taken a great first step and God wants to **hear from you**.

THERE ARE NO MAGIC WORDS YOU HAVE TO SAY TO GOD.

It's more about your heart.

> Can you admit that you've sinned? That even on your best days, you've done things and thought stuff you aren't proud of? Tell God about it.

> Are you sorry for those things? Tell God about it.

> Do you want to be different? Tell God about it.

> Do you want to decide to trust God's plan for you and God's love for you, instead of your own idea of what's best? Tell God about it.

By doing this, placing your faith and confidence in Jesus, **you've made peace with God**. And you can continue to understand and experience this peace with God by putting all you have learned over the past four weeks into practice!

If you just decided to follow Jesus by trusting Him, **congratulations!!!**

News like this wasn't meant to be kept to yourself. Talk with your small group leader or student pastor. Talk with your parents, or a good friend. Tell someone about this big step so they can celebrate you, and be there for you on this new journey.

Now you really are at the end of this book. But if you have just decided to start a relationship with God, you are at the beginning of something you will spend your whole life figuring out. It's a journey you won't regret. Because like everything else you've read about the past four weeks, *you are wired for it.*

· WORKS CITED ·
(PROOF WE DIDN'T JUST MAKE IT UP)

1. Ledbetter, Carly. "Science Explains Why Cilantro Tastes Like Soap For Certain People," *Huffington Post*, 15 June 2015. http://www.huffingtonpost.com/2015/06/24/why-does-cilantro-taste-bad-like-soap_n_7653808.html

2. Davis, Katie. *Kisses From Katie: A Story of Relentless Love and Redemption* (New York: Howard Books, 2011). Additional information online at https://amazima.org/about-us/katies-story

3. Petfinder, Pet Microchip FAQS, https://www.petfinder.com/dogs/lost-and-found-dogs/microchip-faqs/

4. Kirschner, Chanie. "Do Babies Dream?" Mother Nature Network. http://www.mnn.com/family/babies-pregnancy/stories/do-babies-dream

5. Davenport, Barrie. "How Positive Thinking Re-Wires Your Brain." http://www.stevenaitchison.co.uk/blog/how-positive-thinking-re-wires-your-brain/

6. Maslow, Abraham H. A Theory of Human Motivation (originally published in *Psychological Review*, 1943, Vol. 50 #4, pp. 370-396).

7. Yudkin, Daniel. "Without Friends Or Family Even Extraordinary Experiences Are Disappointing," *Scientific American*, 27 January 2015. http://www.scientificamerican.com/article/without-friends-or-family-evenextraordinary-experiences-are disappointing/

8. Jaffe, Eric. "Why Dogs Look Like Their Owners," PetWeek, *Fast Company*. http://www.fastcodesign.com/3037279/pet-week/why-dogs-look-like-their-owners

9. Angelle, Amber, "Why Do Couples Start To Look Like Each Other?" *Live Science*, 26 June 2010. http://www.livescience.com/8384-couples-start.html

10. Groth, Aimee, "You're the Average of the Five People You Spend the Most Time With," *Business Insider*, 24 July 2012. http://www.businessinsider.com/jim-rohn-youre-the-average-of-the-five-people-you-spend-the-most-time-with-2012-7

11. Blanton, Brad. *Radical Honesty: How To Transform Your Life By Telling The Truth* (Stanley, Va.: Sparrowhawk Publishing, 2005). Additional information at http://radicalhonesty.com/

12. Zenger, Jack and Joseph Folkman, "The Ideal Praise-to-Criticism Ratio," *Harvard Business Review*, 15 March 2013. https://hbr.org/2013/03/the-ideal-praise-to-criticism

13. Editors of Publications International, Ltd, "11 Longest-running Daytime Soap Operas." http://entertainment.howstuffworks.com/11-longest-running-daytime-soap-operas.htm#page=1

14. Manning, Brennan, *A Glimpse of Jesus* (New York: HarperOne, 2004)

15. Iannone, Jason, "30 Amazing Animals With Secret Abilities You Never Knew About." https://www.distractify.com/30-animals-that-are-secretly-amazing-1197620344.html

16. Russell Stover Customer Service Guide, http://www.russellstover.com/custserv/faqmain.jsp?ruleID=102&itemType=CATEGORY&itemID=178&faqcid=266

17. Shmueli, Sandra, "Flash Mob Craze Spreads," CNN, 8 August 2003. http://www.cnn.com/2003/TECH/internet/08/04/flash.mob/Flash Mob. https://en.wikipedia.org/wiki/Flash_mob

ABOUT THE AUTHORS

RODNEY ANDERSON

Rodney is a pastor, a writer, and a communicator who has been in ministry full-time since 2000. He partners with Orange to develop curriculum for middle and high school students. He is currently the director of singles for all campuses of North Point Ministries. He lives in Roswell, Georgia, with his wife, Sarah, his two boys, Asher and Pace, and absolutely positively no cats.

SARAH ANDERSON

Sarah is a writer and communicator who has been involved in ministry since 2003. She has been with Orange as a lead writer and content creator for XP3 High School curriculum as well as a contributing writer for the Parent Cue blog since 2007. Sarah lives in Roswell, Georgia, and is a big fan of her husband, her two boys, Asher and Pace, and (in her weaker moments) McDonalds french fries.